GIVEN TO _____

FROM _____

DATE _____

A very special gift for a very special graduate

A GIFT FOR THE Graduate

DONALD E. WILDMON

Five Star Publishers
1208 Zentwood
Tupelo, Mississippi 38801

A Gift For The Graduate

Table of Contents

An Open Letter To The Graduate

Dear Graduate:

Well, you have finally made it. All that hard work and study is behind you. That little piece of sheepskin is yours and you are about to leave behind some of the best years of your life. You are embarking upon another voyage, the voyage of venturing beyond the academic world into the everyday work world. There are some things I hope you will carry with you on the voyage. It will mean a better trip for you and for those of us who have to make the voyage with you.

THE FEAR OF THE LORD IS THE BEGINNING OF KNOWLEDGE; FOOLS DESPISE WISDOM AND INSTRUCTION.
PROVERBS 1:7

First, I hope you will carry some common sense with you on the voyage. Classroom learning is good and needed and our world would be all the poorer if we failed to have it, but it just isn't enough by itself. Somehow our world seems to have lost some of this common sense that marked a previous generation. Common sense is hard to define, but I guess it means just thinking things through.

Next, I hope you will carry with you some respect for the rights of your fellow travelers. You see, we are all making this journey together and that means that we can't go it alone. You have rights, and you should protect those rights less someone take them from you. Those rights have come at a great price. Many a fellow traveler has given his life for those rights of yours. So protect them. But at the same time remember that those of us who travel with you also have rights. We are human beings, also, with the same desires and hopes and feelings that you have. I guess the best way you can protect your rights is to respect the rights of others. You see, it's like I said, we are all in this thing together and if the ship sinks we all go down. That includes you.

Also, please remember to take along something to help you with your responsibilities. Responsibilities are kinda like the home work you had to do, it makes the difference when the test comes. And this is where the real problem is today. Everybody wants his rights, yet not everybody assumes his responsibilities. This makes for trouble. If there's a hole in the ship and you don't dip out your share, someone else will have to work twice as hard to keep the ship from sinking. If another person decides he doesn't want to dip his share, then the ship is in real danger of sinking.

Then another thing I hope you will do on the trip is to put in more fuel than you use. You see, there are a lot of folks who don't contribute anything in the way of fuel for the trip. They are just freeloaders. This means somebody else has to contribute their share of fuel for them. And you can remember from the school books that if your fuel runs out the ship stops. So leave a little more than you take.

There's one other thing you will need for the trip and that's a compass. For a lot of times we lose our sense of direction and the result is war, and poverty, moral decline, hate, crime and the other things that would destroy our ship. You see, just by setting sail doesn't mean we are going to arrive at our destination. We need to continually check our charts to make sure we are headed in the right direction. Progress is a good thing, but it just doesn't happen. Someone has to make it happen.

Well, I hope you have a good journey. This is my wish for you not just because you are graduating, but because there have been so many people who have invested so much in you and have done so much to make possible that sheepskin certificate. They include your parents, teachers, friends, and a host of other people who provided funds, and help, and encouragement. They are all pulling for you.

The ship is in your hands now. Chart a good course, set sail, and stay true to the best there is in you.

It Is As You Will

Years ago I ran across a simple little story which contained a world of truth. I would like to share that story with you.

There was an old hermit-philosopher once who lived in the mountains of Virginia. The local high school boys considered the old man a freak and liked to toss fun at him. But the old man, with a wisdom gained from common sense and experienced and tempered by the touch of God, always seemed to prove just a little wiser than his young friends.

Quite often some of the village boys would tempt the old man with puzzling questions. Rarely did any of the puzzles succeed in embarrassing him. One day one of the boys found a bird that was sick and unable to fly. The boy picked the bird up and kept it till it got well. Shortly thereafter some of the boys were trying to devise a good trick to play on the old hermit. Suddenly the boy who had the captured bird hit upon a bright idea.

"Listen," he exclaimed to the others in the crowd, "I have a bird in a cage at the house. I will take the bird in my hands and we will go up to visit the old hermit. I will ask him if the bird is dead or alive. If he says that the bird is dead, I will turn it loose and let it fly. But if he says that the bird is alive, I will crush it."

It seemed like a brilliant flash of superior wisdom to the group of boys. Why had they never thought of anything like that before? Why,

> AND WHEN HE WOULD NOT BE PERSUADED, WE CEASED AND SAID, "THE WILL OF THE LORD BE DONE."
>
> ACTS 21:14

10

it was simply fantastic. Either way the old man answered they had him.

The boy rushed home and took the bird from the cage. Then, as fast as he could run, he hurried back to where the other boys were. Soon the group was formed and together they set out toward the woods where the hermit lived.

As they approached the hermit's hut, most of the boys were giggling and laughing at the trick they were to play on the old man. The thought of making a fool of someone who was different from themselves gave the boys immense pleasure. What a joy it would be to see the hermit embarrassed by a wrong answer.

The hermit was waiting as the boys came up to the hut. He noticed the grins on their faces and prepared himself for something that was supposed to embarrass him.

The boy with the bird in his hands did the talking. "Old man," he said, "you are so wise and we are so dumb. I have a question for you. Tell me, what is this I hold in my hand?" The hermit proceeded slowly with his answer. "Well, my son, it looks like a bird." A cheer went up from the boys as they laughed at the hermit's answer.

"You are right, old man, it is a bird. Now tell me, is this bird dead or alive?" The hermit looked at the bird and then slowly gave a glance at each of the boys in the crowd. Then he looked deep into the eyes of the youth holding the bird and spoke. "It is as you will, my son. It is as you will."

Young graduate, your life is in your hands. Will you crush it or give it wings to fly? It is as you will.

Living Your Own Life

Jesus made up his own mind. He listened to what others had to say, but He reached His own conclusions. And in doing this, Jesus lived His own life. All graduates can learn from this.

One healthy trait each of us needs is this ability to live our own life, to make our own decisions. Many people were critical of Jesus. They criticized what He said and did. But amid all their criticism Jesus did not allow their opinions to adversely influence Him. Jesus lived His own life.

> JESUS PAID
> NO ATTENTION
> TO WHAT
> THEY SAID...
>
> MARK 5:36

One of the most healthy traits of personality one can have is this ability to live his own life regardless of the criticism or opinion of others. How does one acquire this ability to live his own life? There are some guidelines which will help.

In order to live his own life, one needs to expect criticism. We cannot please everyone. It is an impossibility. And the surest way to ruin your mental health is to try to please everyone. It is impossible for us to be "all things to all people." To attempt to do so is a form of certain suicide. In every situation we are going to be criticized regardless of the choice we make.

Too often we base our actions, make our decisions, on what we think others expect us to do. Too many of us are afraid we might do something someone would criticize us for. We make our decisions not on what we think is best – but on our opinion of what others would think or say of our actions. The result is that we are captives of our opinion of society's opinion – unable to deal with situations where we can't make everyone happy. We are in a far better position to face life with a healthy mental attitude if we make our decisions on the basis of what we believe best and not on the basis of others' opinions.

Then, also, if we are to live our own life we need to learn to accept criticism. If criticism is a part of life, and we fail to learn to accept it in the normal flow of living, then we are in for some serious mental trouble along the way.

Many parents teach their children to avoid criticism. What they need to be doing is to teach the children to accept criticism. There is a world of difference between the two—accepting and avoiding. You can accept, but you cannot avoid. To teach a child to accept criticism is to put a goal within his reach. To teach him to avoid criticism is doing serious damage to his personality.

Also, if we are to learn to live our own life there are times when we need to ignore criticism. Mark once stated in his book these words: "Jesus paid no attention to what they said." What wonderful words! There are times when the best one can do is to ignore what others think or say.

We simply must not let the opinions of those who would criticize us rule us or dominate us. There is only one criteria of judgment in every situation – what is right and what is best. And that is what God expects us to do. Be aware of other's opinions, but make your own decision.

We must not fear criticism, but use it if it is valid or ignore it if it isn't. Live your own life and it will be a better life.

Keep Digging

A medical doctor, with a deep desire to write a novel, took his family on vacation to a remote Scottish farm. There he hoped to be away from the normal routine long enough to prepare the novel which had been burning inside him.

While his family enjoyed the wonders of nature, he confined himself to a desk with his pen in hand in an upstairs room. Hour after hour, day after day he struggled with the novel. There were moments when it seemed he was making real progress, but there were also times when his effort seemed like real drudgery.

One day he grew tired and weary of the project, decided in disgust that it was a waste of his time, and reasoned that he should give up the rather stupid idea. He gathered up what he had written and walked to the back door. There he threw the manuscript in the ash heap, for he figured that was where it belonged. Then he went for a walk in the rain.

During the course of his walk he came to a farmer who was digging in a field in an effort to make a pasture. He struck up a conversation with the farmer and told him about his experience with writing. He told the farmer what he had done with the manuscript.

The farmer didn't speak for a moment. Then he said something of real significance to the doctor. "No doubt you're the one that's right, Doctor, and I'm the one that's wrong." He looked hard at the doctor and continued. "My father ditched this bog all his days and never

> SO LET US NOT BECOME TIRED OF DOING GOOD; FOR IF WE DO NOT GIVE UP, THE TIME WILL COME WHEN WE WILL REAP THE HARVEST.
>
> GALATIANS 6:9

14

made a pasture. I've dug it all my days and never made a pasture." The farmer paused, placed his foot on the shovel, and then continued. "But pasture or no pasture, I cannot help but dig. For my father knew and I know that if you only dig enough, a pasture can be made."

The doctor stood there for a moment and thought about what the farmer had said. He then turned around and headed back to the house. Wet from the rain, ashamed of his lack of stickability, and mad at himself, he picked up the soggy manuscript from the ash heap and went into the house. He dried the pages in the oven and went upstairs to his writing room.

Picking up his pen, the doctor went to work writing again –determined that he would finish the novel. It might prove to be a fruitless venture as he had earlier thought, but regardless of the outcome he was going to have the satisfaction of completing the project. He would at least master himself.

Eventually the novel was finished and the doctor and his family left for home. The manuscript was turned over to a publisher. The doctor felt a sense of relief and accomplishment – and a deep satisfaction.

Few worthwhile projects in life come easy. Usually they come as a result of sheer drudgery and hard, continuous work. But, like the farmer said, if you will keep digging a pasture can be made.

That manuscript became a book entitled *Hatter's Castle* and sold more than three million copies. It was the beginning of a great career for Dr. A. J. Cronin. He kept digging and he made his pasture.

When life gets tough, keep digging young graduate, keep digging.

A Modern Day Parable

There is a parable about a man who was traveling down a certain path. He came to a bend in the path, and being in a hurry, he decided to take a shortcut. He knew that he was not familiar with the shortcut which he had decided to take, but reasoned that since it wasn't too far across and that it would save him some time it was worth the risk.

He had traveled off the main path only a very short distance when he discovered that he was in the midst of a bed of quicksand! No wonder other travelers had avoided taking the shortcut. Slowly he felt himself going under.

Worried that he would die before anyone could pass by to help him, his heart leaped for joy when he heard the footsteps of another traveler coming down the main path. Soon the traveler came into view and the sinking man recognized him as Confucius. "Help!" he called out. "Help me. I'm sinking!" Confucius saw him, paused and then remarked: "That should be evidence that men should stay out of such places." With that Confucius continued on his way.

As the man continued to slowly sink into the quicksand, he knew that he would soon be dead. But suddenly there was another traveler on the path. The sinking man recognized the traveler as Buddha. "Help me, Buddha, before I die." Buddha looked at the man and spoke: "Kill the desire to live which you have and you will be alright." Then Buddha continued down the path.

By and by another traveler came down the road. He was Mohammed. As the sinking man cried out for help, Mohammed stopped to survey the situation. Seeing what had happened, Mohammed cried out to the man: "I can do nothing. It is the will of Allah." With that, Mohammed passed on by.

By the time that the quicksand was to the man's waist, a Hindu appeared on the path. In a voice weak from exhaustion the sinking man called out for help. "Please, my friend, help me for I am about to die." The Hindu showed little concern for the man, but he did try to comfort him. "Don't worry," the Hindu called out, "perhaps in the next life you will return to earth in the form of the sacred cow." The sinking man watched as he walked away.

The man had given up hope of survival by this time. The quicksand was up to his shoulders and only one arm and his head were still exposed. But he heard footsteps on the path again. Looking up, he saw that it was Christ walking down the path. In a feeble, broken voice he cried for help. "Sir, I have called to others for help. In their own way each of them did what he believed would be of help to me. Please, sir, unless you help me I shall surely die."

Jesus left the main path, went down to where the quicksand was, and reached out His hand. "Give me your hand, my brother, and I shall pull you out." Together, arm in arm, they walked down the main path.

Remember this parable the next time you are about to go under.

Walking The Rails

Have you ever tried walking the rails? As a youngster growing up I had to walk about a mile to school. The railroad track ran past both my house and the school. It was the shortest and quickest way to go.

I can remember many times while walking to and from school that I would try to walk the rails – seeing how far I could go without falling off. I usually didn't get too far before a foot would slip and I would be off the rail and on the crosstie.

I read once of a group of scouts who happened upon some abandoned railroad track. Each scout took his turn in trying to walk the entire length of the track without falling off. None of the boys were able to go the entire length without falling off.

> A BROTHER HELPED IS LIKE A STRONG CITY, BUT QUARRELING IS LIKE THE BARS OF A CASTLE.
>
> PROVERBS 18:19

Two of the boys got their heads together and after some discussion came running to the group smiling from ear to ear. They told the group that they were willing to bet that they could walk the entire length of the track without falling off.

The others in the group thought it was a good bet because they had already seen each of the boys fail in an attempt to accomplish the feat. So the bet was accepted and the two boys moved toward the track.

Each of the boys got on a separate rail and began their walk. Side by side they were walking down the track. Soon one of them got a little shaky, so the boys stopped. Then they did something none of the other boys had thought of – they each reached out and joined hands! After joining hands they were able to walk the entire length of the track without falling off. Joining hands and supporting each other they were able to accomplish what neither of them could accomplish alone.

When we help another we help ourselves. When we lend a helping hand we receive one in return. Neither of the two boys could walk the length of that track separately. But by joining hands the task was made relatively easy.

How much our world needs to learn this truth – that there comes a time when we need to join hands and support each other in order that we can achieve that which will be mutually beneficial to all concerned. The different races of mankind need to learn this. So do the different nations of the world. And, likewise, so do individuals.

Many communities and businesses have learned this truth. Time was when every man had his own water well. But now we have community water and it is better for all concerned. And many businesses have folded because they refused to cooperate with other businesses for the good of all.

There are many rails in life which graduates have to walk. Some of them are very difficult to master by ourselves. But if we are willing to extend a hand and receive a hand, we will find that walking the rails of life is much easier to accomplish.

Is It Sterling?

Many times in my life I have heard someone speak of silverware, and the question will be asked: "Is this sterling?" I never really knew what the origin of the question was, except that sterling was supposed to be the best type silverware. And, really, I doubt if many of those who asked the question were aware of the origin of the question.

> "A GOOD NAME IS
>
> TO BE CHOSEN
>
> RATHER THAN
>
> GREAT RICHES…"
>
> PROVERBS 22:1A

The word came into our language many years ago because of a silversmith by the name of Sterling. It seems as though many of the silversmiths in those days would defraud the buyer through the use of a baser metal. The buyer, unable to tell the difference, would often pay a large sum for something he thought was solid silver only to find out years later that the silversmith had cheated him.

Sterling was a silversmith who was a man of honesty. People who bought his products could be sure that the product was of high quality and no attempt to defraud the buyer had been made. Because of Sterling's utter trustworthiness, the king engaged Sterling to make all the silverware for the court. He could be assured that if it bore the mark "sterling" it would be genuine in value. And now we all want to know if it is sterling silverware!

A graduate needs to remember that a person is known by his deeds. It is what you do that you are known for more than what you say. Somewhere in that Book among books we read these words: "Their end will correspond with their deeds." I kinda figure that those words are true.

Many centuries ago two men were contemporaries in history. Whether or not they ever came face to face with each other is uncertain. There is a distinct possibility that they did. The two men were named Paul and Nero. Paul was an itinerant preacher, traveling from town to town proclaiming a strange new doctrine about one called the Nazarene. He was the scorn of the respectable people of the day, and sometimes found himself leaving a town in a hurry – often to save his life!

Nero was the ruler of the Roman Empire. He was a great man who ruled all men. He was a member of the respectable section of society. In fact, he even declared himself to be a god!

Centuries have come and gone since Paul and Nero faced each other, if indeed they did. It has been a long time since Nero burned Rome and blamed Paul and the Christians. But somewhere along the way from there to here, men started calling their sons Paul and their dogs Nero.

I have never heard of a modern-day man who had the name Judas. The only usage of the name I have ever heard has been to identify one as a traitor. But before Judas Iscariot did what he did it was quite a common name – well respected.

Like I said, I guess it is true that a person is known by his deeds. And I believe I would rather have others call me Sterling than Nero – or Judas.

The Present Versus The Future

Late on the night of April 14, 1912, the Titanic, the world's largest and most luxurious ship, was steaming at 22 knots about 95 miles south of the Grand Banks of Newfoundland. The more than 2,000 people aboard the ship were all enjoying themselves. They had little to worry about.

After all, the ship was considered "unsinkable." It had a double-bottomed hull which was divided into 16 watertight compartments. Since four of the compartments could be flooded without endangering the liner's buoyancy, hardly anyone suspected there was the slightest chance that the ship could go down.

THE WISE MAN'S

PATH LEADS

UPWARD

TO LIFE...

PROVERBS 15:24A

In the path of the Titanic that night was a huge iceberg. Other ships in the area, as many as five, tried to warn the Titanic of the danger. However, each time a message went through, the Titanic sent back a message stating that they did not wish to be bothered – they were listening to the Cape Race.

The Cape Race was a yacht race held off the Cape of Africa. The story has it that many of the wealthy passengers on board the Titanic had bet money on the race and were interested in the outcome. Thus the radio operator paid no attention to the other ships' warnings.

Suddenly the Titanic struck the iceberg. It ripped a 300 foot gash in the right side of the vessel, rupturing five of its watertight compartments and causing it to sink at 2:20 a.m. on April 15.

After the crash, the radio operator tried desperately to secure help.

The liner Carpathia arrived on the scene some 20 minutes after the Titanic sank and several lives were saved. The liner Californian was less than 20 miles away all night but had no radio operator on duty to receive the stricken vessel's distress calls.

As a result of the crash some 1,513 people died. It was one of the greatest disasters in maritime history. And it was completely unnecessary. Instead of paying attention to where they were going, those responsible were more interested in current attractions.

That is always a present danger in life – that we become so amused with the present that we pay little heed to where we are headed. It is easy to become so involved in present affairs that we hardly think it necessary to see what the future might hold as a result of the course we are following.

It would have saved the lives of those 1,513 passengers had that radio operator taken just a couple of minutes to check the course the ship was following. But a yacht race was immediate, and the immediate was more important or at least more pleasurable – than the future.

Many are there who are so caught up in present pleasures that they take no time to see the results of the course they have charted with their lives. And, like that radio operator and those few wealthy people with bets on a race, they ignore whatever warnings the Church or society may beam their way.

Occasionally it just makes good sense to check the results of the course you have charted. The Titanic proved that. For, like the Titanic, none of us are unsinkable despite the fact that we often think we are.

After you graduate, keep checking the course you have charted for your life.

How Much Did He Leave?

One day two fellows were talking about a rich man who lived in their community who had just died. Everyone around knew the man who had died was very wealthy, having spent his entire life in the pursuit of the dollar. One fellow turned to the other and asked a question nearly everyone was asking: "I wonder how much he left?"

FOR THE LOVE OF MONEY IS A SOURCE OF ALL KINDS OF EVIL...

I TIMOTHY 6:10

It is a question that is asked often. Someone dies, comes to the end of the road, and leaves a large sum of money and others are curious as to the amount he left. Too often the question is asked in an envious way, as if the one asking the question was wishing that he could lay claim to the estate.

Now this brings us around to one of the most important aspects of life – the proper attitude toward money. We don't have to look far in this crazy world in which we live to see that it is needed – this proper attitude toward money – sometimes desperately needed. It is something every graduate could use. For a large percentage of our world's problems are caused by our attitudes toward the green stuff. People have – and continue to do so – killed, robbed, beaten, cheated, lied, and stolen for less than a dollar.

We have to have money to live. That is a hard fact of life. The difficulty comes when some think they have to have more than others, and that the world owes them something.

There is nothing wrong with money, despite what we have been led to believe. For in itself, money is neither moral nor immoral. Money is what the person who has it makes it. It can be used for good, constructive purposes – or it can be used to destroy, cripple, and kill. It depends upon the user.

The Galilean gave us the secret here. Money, He taught, is to be used for the good of mankind. He never condemned the making, honestly, of a large sum of money. He only condemned the misuse of it. He was well aware of the fact that too many people misuse money, become selfish and stingy in their concept of the use of money.

There are a few people who gain from this Carpenter the proper concept toward the use of their money. And they aren't always folks with large sums of wealth. Often they are common people who place what they have into His care and seek to build a better world with it.

We see so many people who are stingy. They hoard and keep nearly everything they get. And if they part with much of it, it is usually spent on themselves. Unfortunately we have reached a social opinion in our country that only rich folks can be stingy. But some of the stingiest people around are those who have very little. You don't have to be rich to be stingy. You only have to have a poor heart. And this is caused by a selfish conception of what money is for.

I mentioned the fact that one fellow asked the other how much the wealthy man left when he died. The second fellow turned to him and answered: "He left all he had." I guess, when it is all over, that's how much each of us will leave.

The Beautiful Building

"See that church building over there," I said to my friend in the car with me. I was pointing off to my left to a building set back off the highway and nestled in a grove of trees. "Very beautiful building isn't it," he remarked. "Yes it is. Or at least it appears to be. There is a sermon in that building," I said. "Yep, the preacher preaches it every Sunday," my friend replied. "Oh, no. I mean the building is a sermon."

> YOUR BEAUTY SHOULD NOT COME FROM OUTWARD ADORNMENT. INSTEAD, IT SHOULD BE THAT OF YOUR INNER SELF...
> 1 PETER 3:3-4 (NIV)

I went on to tell my friend about my first contact with the church building. I was remarking to some people about how pretty the building was one day when they told me that the building was not finished on the inside. I was really surprised because the building appeared to be at least five to ten years old. And when I went in, sure enough, I found that the building was not complete.

"Think about this," I said to my friend. "From the outside of the building everything is beautiful. The people built it that way to at-

26

tract other people to come to it. But inside the building there is a lot of work to be done yet. Once a person sees the inside he forgets about the beauty of the outside."

Is this not what the Fisher of men taught? Not to judge beauty by appearance, but by deeds. Not to look for beauty on the outside, but to take an inward look. Here was the building – a beautiful little church building – that gave the appearance of something you would like to be associated with. But inside was nothing but unfinished work. How many times are our lives like that. We look at someone who looks nice and lovely and comment what a beautiful person she or he is. But when we get to know the person better – when we look behind the beautiful face and splendid clothes – we see an unfinished life.

Many, indeed, are those who have finished the outside structure of their lives. They always dress neat, live in nice and well kept houses, drive a car that is a real eye catcher, and always seem to be in the right company. But inside their lives, down deep where beauty is proved by deeds, they are empty.

A lady called me one day and chewed me out good because the grass on our church lot had not been cut recently. I had to agree with the lady that the grass needed cutting. But this same lady seldom – if ever – darkened the doors of any church building. She was concerned about outside looks and didn't care about the view inside.

Someone has said that beauty is only skin deep. They missed the mark completely. Real beauty can only be found down deep in one's heart. The outside appearance is an illusion.

"And that," I told my friend, "is the sermon."

A Prison Becomes A Home

Bob Bartlett tells of one of his experiences as an explorer. On one trip his party was bringing back a large number of birds. Of course the birds were caged. Bartlett stated that about halfway home one of the restless birds escaped from his cage.

The group watched the bird enjoy his new found freedom, and then they followed him as he flew out across the water out of sight. Some in the group said the bird was lost, that there was no place for him to go.

> HE HAS SENT ME TO
>
> PROCLAIM
>
> FREEDOM FOR THE
>
> PRISONERS...
>
> LUKE 4:18B (NIV)

Several hours later the bird was sighted returning to the ship. Soon it landed – out of breath – on the ship it sought so eagerly to escape. What the bird had considered a prison previously he was now happy to call his home!

Many times this is true –what we consider a prison turns out to be a home. This is especially true with many in the Christian faith. They approach it from a legalistic viewpoint and grow tired of trying to follow its Leader. The time comes when they consider the faith a prison and they desire to be free.

So they open the cage door and set sail for freedom! No longer are they confined to a religion which seems to constrain their desires. The

Galilean Carpenter told a story about such a person once.

The young man was tired of living in his father's home. He desired to be free to live his own life as he pleased – to follow only his own desires. So he asked for and received his share of the family wealth. He packed his bags and headed for new territory where he would be free. No longer would he be caged by the will of his father. Now he could do as he pleased.

But it didn't turn out like the young man thought it would. It never does when we give way to our cheap yearnings. In that new territory the young man had plenty of friends as long as he had plenty of money. At least he thought they were friends. But he found out differently when his money was gone.

When he got to the place where he was wanting to eat even the slop which the pigs he was feeding ate, he thought of home. Home was no longer a prison to him – now it was a heaven. And, lik e the bird that escaped his cage, he soon found himself going back to the place he desired to escape.

How often comes the desire to desert our Christian faith for something less demanding on our will. How often we think freedom can be found in following our own selfish pursuits. But after we leave there comes a time when the prison takes on a new perspective.

The boat was still there when the bird returned. So was the father when the young son came home. They used good logic in returning home. Why die out in the vast of nothingness when we can come home and live?

Often freedom becomes a prison and a prison becomes a home. As a graduate, it will help if you will remember that in years to come.

Determination To Succeed

There was this young boy once. He loved to draw. He would take his pencil and a piece of paper and he would draw anything around him that caught his fancy. Once that young boy was asked to draw a picture of a horse by an elderly gentleman. When he had finished with the drawing the gentleman was so pleased with the boy's work that he gave him a whole dollar! And that was back when a dollar was a dollar.

That seemed to spur the youngster on. He kept drawing. He worked at it. He loved it. He gave himself to it. Soon he had landed himself a job with a newspaper as a cartoonist. He was real proud of himself when he got that job. But while he thought it was something to get excited about, one of his superiors didn't see it that way.

The editor of the paper where he worked in Kansas City called him in one day. He said he wanted to talk to the young man about his future. Being quite frank with the young cartoonist about his job and his future, he said to him: "You don't have any talent. Why don't you get out of the drawing business and into something where you have a chance to succeed?"

Well, the young fellow thought it over. He gave serious consideration to doing just that, quitting his drawing and going into another line of business. For he did want to be a success. And the editor should know about talent. But after considerable thought, he decided to stay in the drawing business even if he didn't "have any talent."

You will find people like that occasionally. People who won't quit, people who won't give up even if others think they are doomed to failure. No one has ever found the magic formula that separates those who refuse to quit from those who give up at the first setback. A lot of time, however, it can be nothing more than the Spirit of the Creator driving them on. For sometimes there is not a single person in this whole world who believes in us other than Him.

That's one of His traits. He believes in us even when no one else does. He believes in us even when we don't believe in ourselves. That's what made Him face that ugly cross. He believed in our goodness when we displayed our sinfulness. He never gave up on us. He still is counting on us to this very day. He is disappointed a lot of times, but He never gives up. When everyone else has counted us out, he is still pulling for us.

That young artist who "had no talent" but wouldn't quit went on to great heights. His enterprises today rake in hundreds of millions of dollars a year. His name was Walt Disney.

No one can remember the name of the Kansas City editor.

Greatness Is Two Feet Taller

Sir Christopher Wren, the builder of St. Paul's Cathedral in London, was a famous architect of the 17th and 18th centuries. Once he was building a church edifice in London when he was severely criticized by a group of jealous architects. He was told that his type of architecture would not support the massive roof he was putting on the building. After much debate and Sir Christopher's insistence that his architecture would easily support the roof, the officials ordered Sir Christopher to put in additional supporting pillars. Sir Christopher, reluctantly and insisting that they were not needed, did as he was ordered.

> PRIDE GOES BEFORE DESTRUCTION, AND A HAUGHTY SPIRIT BEFORE A FALL.
>
> PROVERBS 16:18

Here was the story of a genius in his field who was forced to go against his own conclusions because of the envy of his competitors.

Funny, sometimes, the way jealousy gets into our system. Someone can do something just a little better than we can, someone gets recognized as being just a little more capable than we are, someone rises above us and we seek to pull them down. It seems that if Sir Christopher found a new way to support a roof that his competitors would rejoice with him and learn from him. But such wasn't the case. They turned against him, scorned and laughed and ridiculed him, and sold the public a bill of goods that his way just wouldn't work.

There are many cases like that in history. Someone comes along with something new, different, better, and we unloose our jealousy on him. We are so self-centered that we will not allow ourselves to recognize greatness when it comes. Rather than paying tribute to greatness, we attempt, and often succeed, in pulling the other person down. Galileo knew something about this.

They treated the Fisher of Men that way, you know. He came with a new way, a more excellent method, a clearer revelation of what the Creator was like, and His fellow counterparts sought a way to destroy Him. He won the hearts of a few men but men in His profession turned against Him. He was doing something new, something that He knew would work. He had full confidence in Himself and His work, but jealousy burned in the hearts of the recognized religious leaders. They sought to destroy Him.

Rather than listen to what this Man had to say and see if it was true or not, they closed their ears and would not hear His message and, prompted by jealousy and selfishness, set about to get rid of Him. He was a threat to their position!

Let someone get in front of us and rather than joining them, we try to pull them down. But life never lets anyone climb higher by pulling another down.

Fifty years after Sir Christopher had finished the church building, some painters were doing some repair work on the church. It was then discovered that the additional pillars that Sir Christopher placed in the building missed the roof by two feet!

Greatness cannot be destroyed by jealousy. Greatness is always at least two feet taller!

The Bigness Of Little Things

Little things aren't too important, are they? No, most of the time they aren't. Or at least we don't think they are. Robert Romano of Staten Island would have probably agreed to such a statement about little things up to a short time ago. Then something happened.

Romano was driving home early one day when, at a deserted intersection, his car ran over a small nail in the road. A tire blew, Romano lost control of his car, and it hit a street lamp. The impact bent the street lamp double. The auto careened off the lamppost and snapped off a fire hydrant, causing flooding under the street.

> ...YOU HAVE
> BEEN FAITHFUL
> OVER A LITTLE, I
> WILL SET YOU
> OVER MUCH...
> MATTHEW 25:21

The deluge undermined the intersection, which collapsed, leaving a 50 foot crater in the street. The cave-in ruptured a gas main and police in hip-boots evacuated 17 nearby residents to safety. Luckily, there were no injuries to anyone involved.

Little things not too important? One little nail, at the wrong place at the right time, caused every bit of that to happen. Guess we better say that all little things except little nails aren't too important. But that won't hold water, either. Best we admit the truth and say that little things are important.

We are sorry for all the damage done in the accident caused by the one little-bitty nail, but we are glad it was there. It made us stop and think and get some of our values back in line. It reminded us, in a dramatic way, that little things do count and count a lot.

You know, we will find life that way. Little things counting, I mean. Remember the time we looked over the shoulder of the classmate in front of us and put his work down for our own when we didn't know the answer? It counted, all right. And remember the time we took that first little sip because we wanted to be one of the crowd? It counted. Sure did. And then there was the time when we took that one little, measly dollar with the full intention of paying it back later. That counted, too. Little things, you see, still count in this world. They count because they are important. They may seem too small to be of significance but they count. Sometimes there appear in life little nails which we had not considered important. And we learn, sometimes the hard way, that little things are important. Oh, how important sometimes!

"You have been faithful in managing small amounts, so I will put you in charge of large amounts. Come on in and share my happiness!" That's what He said. And He is the One Who makes little things important. Our job, you see, is to be good caretakers over the little we have. It doesn't really matter in this life how much we have. But it matters a lot how we manage what little we do have.

Are little things important? Ask Robert Romano. Better yet, ask the Galilean Carpenter. Then watch for the little nails in the roadway of life. They are there.

If You Can't Sing, Whittle!

He was a lad in the town of Cremona, Italy, in the middle of the 17th century. Cremona was a musical town and great acclaim was given to those who could sing or play. Wanting to be accepted and given some recognition for his musical talents, he tried singing. His friends called him "squeaky voice" and he soon realized that his singing would never be anything special.

The young lad then tried to learn to play, but his success wasn't much better than his singing. So he was a dejected lad as he walked through the streets of Cremona with his friends and listened to their beautiful voices. About the only thing the lad could do was to whittle on a block of wood with his knife.

> TO EACH IS GIVEN THE MANIFESTATION OF THE SPIRIT AFOR THE COMMON GOOD.
>
> I CORINTHIANS 12:4

One day he was sitting on the edge of the street whittling as three of his friends played and sang beautiful songs for the people passing by. Appreciating the musical ability of his friends, many people dropped some coins into their hands to reward their efforts. One gentlemen stopped longer than many of the others and even asked the friends to sing a song again. After they finished he dropped a coin into the hand of the singer. Then he moved on down the street.

Upon looking, the boys discovered that it was a gold coin! It was quite a piece of money to give a street singer. But the man who gave it could afford to do so. "Who was he?" asked the lad who whittled. "It was Amati," his friend with the beautiful voice replied. "Amati who?" asked the lad. "Nicolo Amati," the friend replied. "He is the greatest violin maker in all of Italy!"

That evening at home the lad thought about the man named Nicolo Amati. He was a man who succeeded in the musical field. But he neither sang nor played! The more he thought about the violin maker, the more he became convinced that he wanted to become a violin maker. He wanted to become the best violin maker in Italy!

Early the next morning the lad hurried off to the home of Nicolo Amati. Inquiring about the way, he sat on the doorsteps after arriving and waited for the great violin maker to come out. When Amati came out, the lad told him that he wanted to become a violin maker and asked Amati if he would teach him to make violins. He explained to Amati that he couldn't sing or play, but that he could whittle. And, more than anything else, he wanted to make violins.

Amati accepted the young lad as a pupil. Day after day, week after week, month after month, year after year the young man studied from the master. In due time his work became known in Cremona, then Italy, and finally throughout the whole world.

We may not have the talent to do some things as well as other people. But God has given each of us a very special talent which, if we develop, can help us help others. Antonio Stradivari found this to be true. Even to this very day men still make music with his violins. And they pay hundreds of thousands of dollars to do so!

Just because you can't sing or play doesn't mean you can't make music.

Be Careful What You Build

One day a very rich man came to a friend of his and told him that he was ready to go on vacation. His friend was a contractor, and he gave the man some plans for a house which he wanted built while he was on vacation. The rich man's friend said that he would be happy to build it, and that he would have it completed when the rich man returned from his vacation. The rich man told the contractor not to spare any expense, and to build it the best he could and he would pay him well.

Soon after the rich man had gone, the contractor began work on the house. From his experience, he knew that the building was going to run into quite a large sum of money. He began to think about how much money he was going to make. Then, slowly, an idea entered his mind. Why didn't he use some inferior material on the inside structure of the house? His rich friend wouldn't know the difference, and it would be four or five years before the inferior material showed up. So the builder ordered second grade material to be used in the structure of the house.

DO NOT BE DECEIVED; GOD IS NOT MOCKED, FOR WHATEVER A MAN SOWS, THAT HE WILL ALSO REAP.

GALATIANS 6:7

After a few weeks of work, the contractor saw the building begin to take shape. He thought about how much more money he was going to make since he had decided to use the second-rate material. Then, one day, he began to think about how much more money he could make if he used imitation material in

38

finishing the house on the inside and also on the outside. He could get some material that looked like first-rate stuff but would cost considerably less than the best material that the rich man had ordered. The more he thought about it, the better he liked the idea. After all, the rich man had plenty of money and he was completely ignorant as far as building knowledge went. So he finished the house using imitation material.

One day the rich man returned from his vacation. He called on his friend the builder and asked about the house. His friend told him that they had just finished the house, and that he would be happy to show him the house if he wished. The rich man said he would.

Arriving at the new house, the builder began to point out the fine points in the building. He explained to his rich friend that no expense had been spared, that everything in the building was first-rate material. Telling his rich friend what the total cost ran to, he explained that the best materials had run the cost up as opposed to other homes similar to this one. The rich man said he understood, and that he had expected to pay more. Then he surprised the builder.

"John," he said, "we have been friends for a long time. I have looked for some way to express my love for you and your family. I'm getting on in years and I wanted to do something for you before I die. When we get back to the house, I'm giving you not only a check for the house you have built, but the keys and deed as well. You built it, now you can live in it."

Well, that's the way life is. We build them and then have to live in them. That's the reason we should be careful what we build. You see, there is nothing worse than living in a rotten house.

Playing Second Best

There's a game that most of us need to learn how to play. It's a real exciting and rewarding game. And it is a game that nearly every person can play with good results. The name of the game is "How To Play Second Best."

Now it's true that this game isn't a very popular one. Most of us don't like to play second best because most of us want to lead the parade. And it's nothing wrong, basically, with wanting to lead the parade. We wouldn't be worth much if we didn't want to be at the front of the march. But this is where playing the second best comes in. For any school child can tell you that a parade can only have a very limited number of leaders. The rest must follow.

SIMON, WHO HE NAMED PETER, AND ANDREW HIS BROTHER...

LUKE 6:14A

The real trouble comes when we don't get to lead the parade and must become one of the followers. Not many of us know how to do that and do it well. Too many times we let our disappointment turn into bitterness and we become critical of the one who is leading.

All of us have experienced this, having to play the role of second best. Fact about the business is that every one of us must do it every day. No person can be a leader in everything. Every person must follow in some things.

There were two brothers once who were commercial fishermen. One brother was a natural leader, the other brother was destined to always be second best. Wherever the two were introduced the introduction went something like this: "Meet Peter, and his brother Andrew. They are fishermen." Andrew was always the last one introduced. Even when Andrew was not with his leader brother Peter, he was still introduced like this: "Meet Andrew, the brother of Peter." No matter where Andrew went he was always second best, always Peter's brother.

But playing second best didn't destroy Andrew. He knew how to play the game and played it like a pro. And anyone who knows the story about these brothers knows that Peter was what he was because of Andrew.

There are some truths that we need to learn in order to play the game of playing second best. First of all, second best doesn't necessarily mean one of smaller stature or of less importance. The running back, quarterback or receiver does the scoring and gets the publicity, but he will be the first to tell you of the worth of the men up front.

Then, too, being second best doesn't mean we haven't done our best. And if a man does his best no one can ask him to do more regardless of what others are able to do. Real judgment comes not from comparing us against another, but comparing our results against our potential. For it is quite evident that all of us do not have the same number of talents.

Andrew played this game like few people can. The thing that made Andrew great while playing second best was his deep-rooted humility. And unless you have that virtue you will never be able to play the game at all.

Uncommon Common People

Something unusual happened over in Zurich, Switzerland, at a theater. A man named Anton Sergeivitch Tartarov gave a piano concert. The billboards said that Tartarov was a great Russian pianist, internationally known. And at the theater Tartarov received a standing ovation and cheers and shouts for encores from the two thousand people present.

AND THE GREAT THRONG HEARD HIM GLADLY.

MARK 12:37B

This concert ended a little different than most of them do, however. When the crowd finished cheering and the impresario stepped up to speak, he told those present that Tartarov was not really Tartarov, that there was no such person, that he was not really Russian but Swiss, and to further complicate matters that the numbers he had played were not the announced numbers of Beethoven, Prokofieff and Liszt but the arrangements of the piano player who was named Jean-Jacques Hauser!

Well, the crowd loved him just the same and still wanted the encore. He gave it to them and was glad to do it. The man who was responsible for the whole show told the people that he "invented

Tartarov to give Hauser an audience free of prejudices."

The story is uncommon, but it shouldn't be. It should be an everyday experience. You see, most of us who think we are common people have some uncommon talent that we can do well –sometimes better than anybody else in the whole world!

And that brings us around to the Galilean. He brought out the greatness in common people. Someone has said that is what got Him placed on that Cross. But He accepted men free of the prejudice that we so often have. He lifted the common man, made him important, even made him great – as a servant.

If you are wondering why the Galilean did this you must remember that He was Himself a "common man." He was a Carpenter, He made things with His hands. Judging by other evidence, He took pride in His work and people appreciated His craftsmanship. And look at the close followers He selected. All of them were common people!

One day, however, this Carpenter laid down the tools with which he worked on wood and picked up the tools with which He worked on the hearts of men. He went to the common people, spoke a message they "heard gladly," put hope and desire and ambition and love in the heart of the common man. And he hasn't been the same since.

The crowd found that even an "unknown" can have greatness. This is exactly what the Galilean Carpenter has been teaching since the earth started spinning.

Handicaps And Greatness

About 1900 years ago a fellow by the name of Paul wrote that he had a "thorn in the flesh." No one has ever known for sure what Paul's "thorn in the flesh" was, but many seem to think that it was a physical defect. Despite his "thorn in the flesh," or maybe because of it, Paul became one of the most outstanding characters of all history. Now there is not a single one of us who does not have some sort of handicap, or a "thorn in the flesh." Most of us like to blame our shortcomings and failures on that handicap, but we should not. I would like to share a list of people with you who have been bothered by the "thorn in the flesh."

> AND TO KEEP ME FROM BEING TOO ELATED BY THE ABUNDANCE OF REVELATIONS, A THORN WAS GIVEN ME IN THE FLESH...
>
> II CORINTHIANS 12:7

Poverty was the handicap of this man. He was so poor that at the age of 6 he practiced his numbers in a cemetery using tombstones as slates. He became one of the foremost mathematicians of all time. His name was Niccolo Fontana.

Poverty was the handicap of this man, also. He was the orphaned son of an Iowa blacksmith. Later he became wealthy, and served as President of the United States. His name was Herbert C. Hoover.

Deafness was his handicap. And though he composed some of the world's greatest masterpieces, he could not hear his own music. His name was Ludwig von Beethoven.

Blindness and deafness were her handicaps. From the time she was two years old she could neither see nor hear. Yet she remains an inspiration to countless others. Her name was Helen Keller.

A crippled body was the handicap of this man. He was a victim of polio who had a body racked with pain. But he became President of the United States. His name was Franklin D. Roosevelt.

Ill health was his handicap. He was an invalid most of his life and seldom knew a moment without pain. His name was Robert Louis Stevenson.

Ignorance was the handicap of this man. He knew nothing about electricity, but inventions in the field of electricity brought him fame and fortune. His name was Alexander Graham Bell.

Ugliness was the handicap of this lady. She was abused and mistreated as a child. Yet she became one of the world's greatest actresses. Her name was Sarah Bernhardt.

The list could go on and on. Stories of men and women who have overcome handicaps to make a mark in life and leave life a little better than they found it. There is one other similar story I would like to share. His handicaps were disgrace and failure. He was brought up in a little country village on the edge of civilization. He tried preaching but got into trouble with the authorities and was sentenced to die. His execution was that of a common troublemaker. His name was Jesus of Nazareth.

And still we complain because of some little handicap.

Being Yourself

Some time ago a company advertised in New York newspapers to fill a vacancy on its sales force. It seems as though the company was in need of a furniture salesman. Several people answered the ad, more than 1500 in all. One of the applicants turned in what was probably the most usual resume in history.

This particular applicant sent back the following reply. "I am presently selling furniture at the address below. You may judge my ability as a salesman if you will stop in to see me at any time, pretending that you are interested in buying furniture. When you come in you may identify me by my red hair. I will have no way of identifying you. Such salesmanship as I exhibit during your visit will be no more than my usual work-a-day approach. I'll make no special effort to impress a prospective employer."

Well, I think most of us will agree that was, indeed, an unusual reply to an ad. Most of us would have written back, telling of our good points and explaining to the company why they should hire us.

Or, if the prospective employer was going to visit us on the job, we would at least like to know which one he was so we could be on the ball and do an outstanding job. After all, most of us do want to impress the boss.

But here was a man who was willing to be himself. Here was a man who wanted his employer to know exactly the type of salesman he was hiring before he hired him. Here was a man who was confident of his ability. He wasn't showy, or pretentious, or superficial. He may not be the world's greatest salesman, but he did the best he could at all times and he was not ashamed of his best. He could greet, and treat, all men with equal respect regardless of their rank or position.

There's a lesson in this story – a true one – for modern man. When you give your job, and anything else, your best you don't have to apologize because you don't have the talent or gifts or money or position of someone else. When you can take any and every person and treat them as though they are your future employer, you have reached a place in life where life can be enjoyed.

The one thing that caused so much friction between the Carpenter and that group known as the Pharisees was the fact that they tried to put up a front, be something they were not, look down on others. And the one thing that caused His heart to go out to the woman who washed and wiped His feet when others wanted to get rid of her was the fact that she was willing to admit what she was.

Usually, life's best results come from accepting yourself for what you are and then beginning from that point. At least it did for the furniture salesman. We said more than 1500 applied for the job. But do you know who got it? You're right. He sure did!

Follow The Leader

In Kuala Lumpur, Malaysia, a cross-country race was held. The race was to cover a seven-mile course. Two hours after the race had begun, ample time for the runners to cover the course, none of the runners had returned. The officials, fearing that something might have happened, set out in automobiles to find the runners.

The officials found all of the runners six miles away, and sprinting in the wrong direction. Many of the runners had already covered distances of ten miles. A. J. Rogers, the association secretary, said the mixup apparently occurred when the lead runner took a wrong turn at the fifth check point and the rest followed him!

> AND IF A BLIND MAN LEADS A BLIND MAN, BOTH WILL FALL INTO A PIT.
>
> MATTHEW 15:14B

Sometimes this happens. We play follow the leader without knowing where the leader is going. We do things simply because someone else does them. We make our decisions because someone else has made the same decision before us. And while this is not always bad, it most certainly isn't always good.

All of us should be aware of where it is that we are going. One of the greatest mistakes of so many in our society is that they are running as fast as they can, following the man in front of them, trying desperately to catch up, and not knowing where the fellow they are following is headed.

Occasionally someone will come along who will consider where it is that he wants to go. He stops long enough to study where following the man in front will lead. These people make up their own minds about which way the race should be going.

The Galilean was a Fellow like this. There was a full fledged race going when He came upon the scene. All the runners were following the leaders. They were pushing with all they had to keep up, to be abreast, racing with the crowd. The leaders had always run their path, and they never questioned its authenticity. They simply took for granted that the runner in front was going the right way.

Then He came into the race. He saw where those who were supposed to be leading the race were headed, and He knew that was not the path that the Judge had set for the race. So He stopped, took note of the roads, and headed off in another direction. Since he was the Leader in this new direction, those leading the race in the other direction became very angry that He should do such a thing. Why didn't He follow them like all the other runners? Of course, the only thing to do was to belittle Him, and eventually get rid of Him. He could prove dangerous to the course they were leading!

Somehow, this same idea of following the leader that prevailed back then is still around today. If the first car passes an injured individual on the highway, all the others are supposed to do the same. If one person takes a belittles Christian values, all other people who follow do the same. If one person shuns another person of different color, then we all must shun him. It's a game we play. We call it follow the leader.

But you know, I believe I would rather know where I'm going than to be in a hurry to follow the man in front of me.

Who Is My Neighbor?

Davis Fulp of Cecil, Georgia, came upon an automobile stalled on a railroad crossing. Its occupant was Rudoph Blanchard, a victim of arthritis who could not get out of his specially built automobile without help. Fulp rescued Blanchard, and they went for help in efforts to remove the car from the tracks. By the time they returned, the automobile had been demolished by a train. Davis Fulp had saved Rudolph Blanchard's life.

Three weeks later, Davis Fulp found himself in a situation in which he needed help. Fulp was walking around a small pond just off Interstate 75 near Cecil when he stepped on a broken bottle and cut a main artery. He managed to get on the highway in hopes someone would help him. He lay on the highway, signaling for help. Cars zoomed by. One stopped. The driver looked at Fulp lying on the pavement. "I held up my leg and both hands," said Fulp. "Blood was pouring from my foot. I said, 'Mister, please help me. I think I am bleeding to death.' "

> BUT HE, DESIRING TO JUSTIFY HIMSELF, SAID TO JESUS, "AND WHO IS MY NEIGHBOR?"
>
> LUKE 10:29

The motorist looked at Fulp, listened to his plea for help, and then drove on. Finally another Cecil resident, Jackie Stalvy, stopped and took Fulp to the hospital.

Seems almost inhuman that one man could see another bleeding profusely, listen to his plea for help, and then drive away without doing a thing. Yet it happens. Every day similar incidents happen.

It is not a new story, this refusing to help those who are in need. A couple of thousand years ago, a Carpenter told a similar story. He said there was a certain man that was traveling from Jerusalem to Jericho who ran into some robbers. They beat him, took his goods, and left him on the road. After a while a fellow came along, and seeing the man beaten and bleeding passed right on by. Soon another fellow came by, saw the man in his misery, probably listened to the man crying for him to help, and then kept walking. Not everyone who passed by was that inhuman however. A fellow who was supposed to be an enemy of the injured man had compassion on him, healed his wounds the best he could, and then carried him to the hospital. And to top it all off, he paid for his expenses while he was healing!

These stories are two thousand years apart in time and yet they are timeless. One happened in Georgia, the other was told in a little country called Samaria. The Man relating the second story was telling what one should do to be a neighbor.

There are people who think of a "neighbor" as a person next door. Had the man who drove off known Mr. Fulp, he would probably have helped in every way he could. Then there are people who think of someone who needs help when the word "neighbor" is used. The Nazarene Who told the story and the lawyer who had asked for a definition of the word both left thinking of a neighbor as one who needed their help.

I wonder which person you would like to meet you on the road if you needed help, the fellow who thought of his neighbor as the person next door or the Fellow Who thought of his neighbor as a person in need?

"Go thou and do likewise."

Life Isn't Easy

One thing one learns about life rather early is that it isn't meant to be easy. From the moment the baby leaves the protection of the mother's security, it begins to cry. And from that moment on life never lets up on its demands on those who try to take it seriously.

FOR THE GATE IS NARROW AND THE WAY IS HARD, THAT LEADS TO LIFE, AND THOSE WHO FIND IT ARE FEW.

MATTHEW 7:14

There are two attitudes one can take toward life. One is the take care of myself, don't care too much about the other person, don't get too involved attitude. This is by far the most traveled road of life for the simple reason that it places no demands upon us that we don't want it to. We can do as we please, or not do as we please. We are content just to live our lives out, patting ourselves on the back, telling ourselves we are doing all that we should be doing.

There is another attitude toward life. That attitude says life is a sacred trust, given to us by the eternal Father, and that it should be used for the benefit of Him and our fellowman. This way of living is very demanding. Very few are there who are willing to strive toward this life. It places demands upon us that we don't want, causes us to strive toward what the masses call the impossible. This is often a very lonely way of living, since those who have common goals are few in number.

Often we are tempted to give up, to call it quits, to say with the carefree lot that it is an impossibility to live toward that high calling. We are tempted to lower our goals, tone down our plea, and think more about ourselves.

But then we ultimately come back to this – life isn't supposed to be easy. It is supposed to be a challenge. And the very moment we cease working toward that high calling, we begin to deteriorate into nothing but a self-satisfied, selfish human that joins the don't care crowd.

When we get to the place where we are ready to throw in the towel and call it quits, what we really need is to know that what we are doing has some significance and lasting value to it. For as long as a person can believe that what he is doing has God's stamp of approval on it, he can face any obstacle that stands before him. But once he quits believing in his high calling, he is doomed to a life of selfishness.

Sometimes the night gets dark, awful dark. And you begin to question whether or not you should forget that high calling. For your job becomes hard, and you see very little chance of it getting any easier in the future. In times like that the only thing that will sustain one is the knowledge that what he is doing has God's approval, that his efforts will not be in vain, and that his God will gladly pour out His grace on those who need it.

Life is easy only when we are selfish. It is hard when we choose the high road. And while it gets to be awful dark sometimes on the high road, we need to remember that daylight always follows darkness.

It's Where You Are

Some time ago I read in the papers an account of a man in Phoenix, Arizona, who had rented an apartment but couldn't move into it because he had lost it! Actually, he couldn't find it. It seems that Charles Rowland had sold his photo-finishing business in Appleton, Wisconsin, and moved to Phoenix. Upon his arrival in Phoenix Rowland checked into a hotel. That same day he found an apartment and paid one month's rent in advance. However, he drove away without noting the address.

After 14 hours of driving around the city to locate the apartment, he notified a local newspaper of his plight. The fellow who had rented the apartment to Rowland read the article and called him at the hotel. It seems that the apartment was just two blocks, a couple of minutes, away from the hotel!

> "HE WHO GIVES HEED TO THE WORD WILL PROSPER, AND HAPPY IS HE WHO TRUSTS IN THE LORD."
>
> PROVERBS 16:20

Then there was the case of Dr. Ellis Shenken, an ophthalmologist in Toronto, Ontario, Canada. Dr. Shenken was punched in the eye and as a result he lost one of his contact lenses. Dr. Shenken, unable to find the lens, got fitted for another soon thereafter. But the eye in which Dr. Shenken got punched kept discharging and his new lens kept popping out. It should have. You see, the lens which Dr. Shenken searched for but couldn't find had been pushed into his eyelid, where it remained unnoticed!

While a student in school, I worked in a grocery store to help defray my expenses. As I was stocking the shelf one day a gentlemen kept walking up and down the aisle looking for some product. Finally, he stopped in the section where the product should be located. After looking for quite a while for the product, he asked me if I knew where the product could be found. Reaching to the spot where he had been looking for several minutes, I picked up the product and gave it to him. His comment? "If it had been a snake it would have bitten me."

It wasn't long after that till I began a search early one morning for my glasses. After searching for several minutes about the house and failing to find them, I began to accuse one of the children or my wife of misplacing them. Seeing I was about to lose what little temper I had, Lynda started searching with me. She came into the room where I was searching and started to speak, only to have a wide grin come across her face. "Go look in a mirror," she said. I took the hint and suddenly realized that I was wearing the glasses I had so desperately been hunting!

Isn't it rather funny sometimes how we can search high and low for something, and then end up finding it in a place where it should have been so simple to find? These four stories could be multiplied by countless individuals who have searched for something only to find it in a place so close by.

Now there is a truth here that could be applied to countless realms. But for the sake of simplicity, let's try just one. Happiness. It's right where you are, if you can find it.

The Greatest Part
Of The Faith

I made what was, to me, a startling discovery recently. I was reading about what happened on that Good Friday in Jerusalem a couple thousand years ago. I read again how they hung that Man among men on those two sticks of wood. I could feel the blows of the hammer as they drove the nails into His palms. I could feel the jar as the cross was dropped into its hole, and came to rest with a terrific jolt. The flesh ripped, and blood spurted.

AND HE SAID TO THEM, "GO INTO ALL THE WORLD AND PREACH THE GOSPEL TO THE WHOLE CREATION."

MARK 16:15

You remember the rest of the events. You remember how the crowd jeered at Him, made fun of Him, jokingly dared Him to come down. It was a scene that has been repeated often in the history of mankind. Over and over again that lowly Galilean has been nailed to those two pieces of wood. Many times we have stood around jeering at Him, making fun of His claims, slashing His side with our selfish spears.

But you can remember, also, that the story didn't end on that dark day. Finding an unused tomb in a garden nearby, they laid Him in it. And then, because the next day was an especially holy one, hardly anyone moved. But Saturday is always followed by Sunday, and on Sunday those who loved Him found what all who have loved Him since have found – an empty tomb.

I said I recently made what was to me a startling discovery. All my life I had thought of that cross and that empty tomb as the most dynamic events in history. I had always considered these as the top jewels to place on a crown of greatness. But now I see that they weren't the greatest part of His Faith. Now I can see that for all these years my sight just did not go far enough to find the most tremendous event in the history of mankind. Now I can see what the greatest part of this Carpenter's Faith is. And it is amazing!

He entrusted the work of His Church to those eleven men, those disciples, who had just prior to the resurrection betrayed Him! That, without a doubt, is the grandest thing about Him —that He trusted common people with the responsibility of His Church! Can you see that? Can you understand what it means? That He should give the greatest responsibility ever known to mankind to these eleven men is without question the highest sign of His love and trust in mankind.

He entrusted His Kingdom not to the high and mighty, to the great and gallant, to the brave and brilliant – but to common people! And He goes on entrusting His Church to common, plain, ordinary folk!

How great His trust in us! That He should give to plain folk the tremendous privilege of carrying on His Work speaks to His great trust in the common man! No one would have dared to trust those eleven men with such a great responsibility except that Nazarene. No one else has such a trust in common folk like you and me.

Next time you are inclined to lose hope in mankind, give it a thought.

Using The Second Best

Back several years ago there was a boy up in Decatur, Illinois, who was very much interested in photography. He ran across an ad in a magazine that offered a book that told all about photography for only a quarter. He sent his quarter to the address that was listed and waited for his book on photography to return.

"AND WHEN THEY HAD COME OPPOSITE MYSIA, THEY ATTEMPTED TO GO INTO BITHYNIA, BUT THE SPIRIT OF JESUS DID NOT ALLOW THEM; SO, PASSING BY MYSIA, THEY WENT DOWN TO TROAS."

ACTS 16:7

The folks at the other end of the line made a mistake, however. Instead of sending him a book on photography as he had ordered, they sent him another one. This one was entitled "A Manual on Magic, Mind-Reading, and Ventriloquism." Well, most of us would have fussed and fumed and written back and let the business house have a good tongue lashing without ever looking at the book.

But the youngster didn't do it like we would. He opened the book and found the section on ventriloquism very fascinating. He began to practice "throwing his voice." Well, sir, he kept practicing and before long he became pretty good at it. Fact about the business is that he became very good at it.

He made himself a dummy to use the "thrown voice" with and then set out on his trail to entertain people. Before long millions of people were listening to those two on Sunday nights and later were viewing them on television. What had begun as a bad break ended up as a way of life for Charlie McCarthy.

All of us could profit from such information. Most of us don't find life to be exactly like we ordered it. Sometimes the breaks seem to go against us. Sometimes we order books on photography and are sent books on magic. But the test in life comes with what we do with what we have to do with.

There was a fellow named Paul who wanted very much to go to a place called Bithynia, but was prevented and went rather to a place called Troas. He didn't get what he wanted but he used what he did get to his and others' advantage. And using it he was able to change the course of the world.

Most of us have to live like that. We have to do with what we have to do with. Sometimes it is a second choice, or third, or even farther down the line. Very rare, indeed, is the person who gets exactly what he wants in life.

There was a song a few years ago that was popular that went something like this: "Do what you do do well, boy. Do what you do do well." Well, it is a good philosophy of life in that little tongue twister. We can't all do what we want to do, but we can all do what we do do well.

Now this brings us around to a Cross. The Book tells us plainly that He didn't want that Cross. But He took it, mastered it, used it, and is conquering the hearts of humans with it. He didn't get what He wanted, but He used what He got.

When life hands you a lemon, the thing to do is to make lemonade.

On Being Rich

Somewhere I ran across the story of a man who visited a certain home. The home wasn't much to look at, kinda run down and needing a good coat of paint. Outside the home, in the yard, a little boy and his sister were playing. They were laughing, and running, and having a good time. The man surveyed the situation, summed up that the family wasn't very well off.

> FOR LIFE IS MORE THEN FOOD, AND THE BODY MORE THAN CLOTHING.
>
> LUKE 12:22

He asked the small boy some questions about the home and family. The little boy told him that his father had not been able to work lately because of illness, and that his mother had to care for the father. When asked about his patched clothes and his bare feet, the youngster explained that he had not had any new clothes since his daddy got sick. After a long period of conversation, the visiting gentleman found out that the little boy and his sister had not been to a movie, or to get a cone of ice cream, or any of the normal accepted childhood pleasures for several months. Wanting to say something to help the boy and his sister face the difficult situation, the man spoke. "It must be awful bad to be poor." Quick as a flash the youngster answered back. "Mister, we ain't poor. We just ain't got no money."

How true! How eternally true! He was happy. He loved his sister. His parents loved him. He knew why his family was in the shape it was in financially, and he didn't complain. Money could not have bought what he had.

How very shallow our judgments go sometimes. How very misplaced our values of riches. We think the only rich people are the people who have money. How miserable life would be if we had to face it on that basis – being poor if we had no money.

We've made a terrible mistake here. And we have passed it on to our children. That mistake is thinking a person has to have a bankroll in order to be rich. What a poor, pitiable basis from which to judge richness. No man is poor who has character, and purpose, whose life has been touched by the Galilean Carpenter, who has love of God and love of fellowman. Every man is poor who lacks those things regardless of his bank account. Whoever uplifts civilization, though he die penniless, is rich, and future generations will erect a living monument to him in deeds. A great bank account can never make a person rich and often hides real richness from him.

A man is rich or poor according to what he is, not according to what he has. We are important because we are God's children, not because of position, or power, or money. No man is rich who has a poor heart. One of the first great lessons of life is to learn the true estimate of values. How poor are those whose major goal is a growing bank account. A rich mind and a noble spirit will cast over the humblest person a radiance of beauty which most millionaires will never know.

Don't pity the person who is lacking money. Pity only the person who is lacking in character, and purpose, who rejects the Galilean, and the Father, and has no love for his fellowman. For they are the poor ones. But those who are the opposite are rich far beyond the expression and means of mortal money.

Persistence

There is a story told about a certain little boy who wanted a watch. Day in and day out he pestered his parents about getting him a watch. His parents put him off every way they could. Finally he drove his parents to the breaking point. His father told the youngster that he didn't want to hear another word about a watch from him.

Well, for the rest of that week the lad said nothing about a watch. He knew that to do so would certainly bring some discomfort to his sitting down place. However, Sunday soon rolled around and the family was gathered together for a period of devotion. It was the custom in the family for each member to learn a new verse of scripture and to recite it each Sunday during devotions. Every other member of the family had said their scripture verse when it came time for the small lad to quote his. Looking up with a very solemn face, he quoted his verse perfectly. "What I say unto you I say unto all, watch." Well, I'm not certain if he got his watch or the other thing. But one thing I can say for him – he was persistent.

And that's a quality all of us could use – persistence. F or one of

> AND LET US RUN WITH PERSEVERANCE THE RACE THAT IS SET BEFORE US...
>
> HEBREWS 12:1B

our faults today is that we give up too soon, call it quits after a single setback, let failure break us instead of make us.

There is very little a person cannot do in this life if he sets out to do it and stays with it. One reason we don't accomplish more is that we are quick quitters. We get a setback or two and then we say it can't be done. We give up. We quit trying. But history is full of things that couldn't be done. And that means it is also full of people who did them.

The world looks up in admiration to a person who has staying-power. He doesn't have to have great brains, or great riches, or vast opportunities. But if he believes in something, and has the persistence to stay with that belief regardless of the praise or scorn he receives, the world ultimately will look up to him.

One reason there aren't any more people with persistence than there are is the simple reason that it takes a big person to try again, or to stick out the ship when the waves get high. Anyone can quit. Anyone can get into a lifeboat and float to safety. But the man with persistence is hunting neither safety nor another mission. He has something he wants to do, and he believes he can do it. So he stays with it, come what may. Then one day he finally accomplishes the impossible.

Great and good goals aren't easy to accomplish. They require great and good people to accomplish them. And great and good people are individuals who keep on keeping on. I believe God wants a person who says, "I can." I believe God wants a person who will try again.

"All things are possible…" He is waiting to see if you believe Him. If you do, try again.

Extra If Assembled

I was in a department store once and noticed several new bikes on display. Since Timmy had asked for a new ten-speed, I decided to look at them closer. I noticed the price tag on one of the bikes. Underneath the price, in small print, was written *$5 Extra If Assembled*.

I started thinking about that - about how much that extra line applied to life. For life, you see, is like the bike - you have to pay extra to get it assembled. Life never comes assembled, even though we quite often wish it would. How easy it would be, we often think, if life came assembled in a neat package ready for instant use. But the truth of the matter is that it doesn't.

Each individual has to assemble his own life, put it together himself. And, like the bike in the store, we have to pay extra for the assembling. Now if the person who puts that bike together follows the directions which come with the package, that bike will provide years of service and withstand the bumps in the road over which it will have to be ridden.

ALL SCRIPTURE IS INSPIRED BY GOD AND PROFITABLE FOR TEACHING, FOR REPROOF, FOR CORRECTION, AND FOR TRAINING IN RIGHTEOUSNESS, THAT THE MAN OF GOD MAY BE COMPLETE, EQUIPPED FOR EVERY GOOD WORK.

II TIMOTHY 3:16-17

Life is like that, also. Put your life together following the Manufacturer's guideline and you will be able to meet the bumps in life's road without being damaged. Of course, if you pay no attention to either the instructions concerning assembling the bike or your life, you can expect trouble trying to make either operate correctly.

The Man of Galilee gave us the clue when it comes to putting our life together. "Seek first God's way," he said, "and the rest will fall into place." Despite many efforts, a better approach toward assembling life has not been found.

We are given life - but not as a finished product. We have to put some effort into it if it is ever to work right. You wouldn't dare take that box of unassembled bike parts, shake it good, and expect the bike to fall out of the box completely assembled and ready to use. Why, then, should one expect life to fall into place automatically? It is extremely more delicate and has far more pieces to be fitted together than the bike.

If you life hits more and more bumps which are becoming rougher and rougher, it is probably because you have failed to follow the instructions in attempting to assemble it. You can, with your life as with the bike, reassemble it if it wasn't put together right to begin with.

And it is foolish to think that your life will automatically correct itself any more than the bike will. You have to expend an effort and follow instructions if you expect your life, or your bike, to be ready to meet the rough places in the road.

Personally, I want my bike and my life to be able to take the bumps. For that reason, I try to follow the instructions given by my Manufacturer as closely as I follow those of my bike's manufacturer. To me, it just makes good sense to do so.